Quilt

inspired by **Máximo Laura**

quilted by Rosalind Johansson

Dedication

This book is dedicated to my mother, Connie Fairey, who, as well as many other creative pursuits, enjoyed her role as wardrobe mistress for her very active local amateur dramatic group, almost until her death in her late 80s .

Her encouragement to the creative in myself, and my children has given us lifetimes of joy and self expression, and we can only thank her from our hearts for her nourishing of those seeds .

Published by Rosalind Johansson 2023
Shorelines Studio, Maitland Place, Finstown, Orkney KW17 2EQ

ISBN 978-1-912889-36-5

© Rosalind Johansson and Máximo Laura

Printed by The Orcadian, Hatston Industrial Estate, Kirkwall, Orkney KW15 1GJ

Contents

Introduction	01
Máximo Laura, a life in weaving	03
Andean symbolism in Máximo's work	09
Rosalind Johansson, my journey	17
Materials, fabrics and haberdashery	24
Step by Step - Project 1. The Beloved	26
Step by Step - Project 2. Conciliation	33
Gallery: tapestries and quilts	50
Design templates	75
Acknowledgements	94
About the Author	95

Introduction

This book centres on the art of quilting, with it's special focus on translating the designs of Peruvian Master Weaver, Máximo Laura, onto the quilted canvas.

You might be wondering, why dive into the realm of tapestry weaving when you're a quilter? A fair question.

Take a moment to explore Máximo's world - the enchanting, vivid tapestries that he conjures.

Allow his designs to paint a picture in your mind, to weave stories of their own. Once you've witnessed the magic, you'll find yourself captivated, drawn into a realm that's both mesmerising and irresistible.

Within these pages lie a treasure trove of opportunity. Máximo's generosity shines through, as he shares a selection of his designs, inviting you to embrace them as your own.

It's a chance to embark on a journey into the heart of Andean cultures and their spiritual expressions. Here, Máximo's inspiration becomes your guiding light, illuminating a path to quilts that sing!

Máximo Laura
a life in weaving

A Quilting book about a weaver?

A little unusual, but this is not just any weaver.

To those not familiar with the work of Máximo Laura, I enclose an introduction from his website (with permission of course), and then, to provide the real context of his work, I call upon the skill of Jayne Bentley Gaskins, who graciously gave her permission for me to use the excellent article she wrote for Fibre Art Now magazine in 2013, which I have updated and interspersed with some observations of my own.

Prepare to be delighted by the treasures of Máximo's work within, and the truly astounding contribution he has made to South American culture, enchanting us all.

Máximo Laura (Ayacucho Peru), is an award-winning tapestry weaver, internationally recognised as one of South America's pre-eminent and most unique textile artists. He is a consultant, designer and lecturer on art and contemporary Andean textile design. His work is the integration and synthesis of ancestral weaving techniques, symbols, memories, myths and rituals with contemporary art.

Laura is the fifth generation of weavers that learnt his craft as a child at the side of his father while growing up in Ayacucho. He learned his art by never silencing the internal self-exploration, or the external exploration of the world, including a lifelong study of art history and literature beyond the borders of Peru .

While he now lives and works in Lima, his work is deeply imbued with the legends and storytelling of his Peruvian heritage, and with his own very compelling life experiences. Laura draws on many sources of inspiration, such as the Chavin culture, which is expressive and totemic; Paracas which is colourful and strong; Nasca and Huari for their geometric forms, and Chancay for its sobriety and linear spirit.

Máximo Laura's vision proposes the promotion of Peruvian contemporary textile art on the international stage, which has been the underlying and fundamental purpose of his artistic mission for the last 30 years.

Owners of Laura's work include the World Bank in Washington DC, the UNESCO headquarters in Paris, the Smithsonian's National Museum of the American Indian, the Museum of Ibero-American craft in Spain, the Museum of the Americas in Miami, the Latvian National Museum of Art and the National Museum of Peruvian culture.

Since his first exhibition at the cultural centre of Buenos Aires, Argentina, in 1985, the work of Máximo Laura has been in over 140 exhibitions in more than 29 countries, (China, USA, France, Italy, Poland, Belgium, Australia, Cuba, Argentina, among others), with solo exhibitions at the Musee de Bibracte, France, the Smithsonian's National Museum of the American Indian. (USA) the Textile Museum (USA), the Museum of the Americas (Costa Rica), the Museum of Decorative Arts and Design (Latvia), the Craft Museum of Finland among others.

Máximo Laura is co-founder of the Iberoamerican Textile Network and the Peruvian Centre of Textile Art. He is also a member of the American Tapestry Alliance, the European Tapestry Network and the British Tapestry Group.

His work has earned many awards, including "National Living Human Treasure" of Peru, "Manos de Oro", (Golden Hands) of Peru, "National Amauta of Peruvian Craft", "Master of Iberoamerican Craft" and the UNESCO prize for Latin America .

Jane Bentley Gaskins article gives us the context and background of Máximo's work

Máximo Laura gives ancient Andean culture a voice of today

In many villages throughout Peru, time has stopped. Indigenous people proudly wear traditional clothing that identifies their specific region and community and they weave and dye the cloth using techniques developed by their ancestors thousands of years before them. At the same time there is another voice in Peru, it comes from Master Weaver, Máximo Laura, who takes the iconography of his heritage and envolves it into the 21st-century through his tapestries. His work translates the spirit of his culture into the world of today.

Máximo Laura is an internationally recognised, award-winning, tapestry weaver, and one of South America's most respected textile artists, consultant and teacher. His work can be found in private and corporate collections throughout the world.

Moreover, the Peruvian Ministry of Foreign Trade and Tourism has awarded him Peru's highest honour in the arts, Amauta, a title, that goes back to the Incan Empire, meaning "wise counsellor". Despite all these accomplishments, Máximo Laura is incredibly humble and unpretentious.

Peruvian weaving through the ages

To understand Máximo's art, you must first understand the world from which it evolved. This entails stepping back in time to the small villages throughout the Peruvian Andes where art has been a principal means of communication for centuries. Spanish is Peru's official language, but the native languages of Quechua and Aymara are still spoken throughout the country. Seldom written, both vary between regions and communities. Art is therefore a vital communication tool. The symbols and motifs displayed in the weavings and other art objects convey the essence of their culture, religion and history.

When the Spanish invaded in the 1500s, they destroyed much of the indigenous culture and forced their religion and way of life on the indigenous people. Recognising the power of communication through art, one of the many indignities imposed on the local people was forbidding them to weave tapestries other than rugs for churches. Everything in their lives, including art and clothing changed to reflect the dictates of the Spanish.

As with most oppressed people, the early Peruvians kept their ancestral religion and history alive secretly through stories and art representing their spiritual and cultural values. These were passed down from generation to generation. Resentment of what they had been denied grew, and they fought for, and won independence in the 1800s. After the revolution, it became safe to resurrect what was left of the old way of life and a new art emerged paying homage to the ancient culture. The Spanish influence, however, had taken a stronghold, and the result was an amalgamation of cultures.

As time passed, pre-Columbian textiles, gradually reappeared and can be seen today throughout the country, but with new twists. Many of the clothes are now adorned with buttons and sequins, much embroidery is done on sewing machines and knitters often use reconstructed bicycle spokes for needles. Some ancient ways, however, have not been lost. Shepherds, tending herds of camelids - alpacas, llamas and vicuñas, protect them from predators, with sling braids that date back centuries.

Whilst llamas and alpacas provide the everyday yarns for clothing and household fabrics of all descriptions, the fibre of the vicuña is one of the most expensive in the world due to its extreme softness, warmth and scarcity. Sling braids are unfortunately no protection against the submachine toting criminals, who arrive in the remote highlands, by motorbike, where the vicuña thrive, to kill and skin the animals. Any villager who tries to intervene also risks being shot .

The animals are shorn and the wool is spun with spindles similar to ones used by their ancestors thousands of years before the Inca. It's a common sight to see Peruvian men and women on the side of the road, spinning wool and cotton, with handheld spindles. Idle moments are never wasted.

While textile factories can be found in major cities, the backstrap loom is still the only method of weaving cloth in the highlands. Traditionally, the spun fibre is first dyed with natural dyes and fixed with natural mordants. Next the yarn is warped on a backstrap loom for weaving. These beautiful textiles are incredibly time-intensive. For example it takes a month to weave a detailed piece about 5' x 18". Textiles and other arts are often produced in family units where everyone contributes and the techniques are passed on from generation to generation.

Regrettably, some of the more intricate designs and processes are in danger of being lost as they are not written down, but remembered by the weavers. Often tourists who are ignorant of the quality and value of textiles made by ancient techniques are unwilling to pay fair prices. As a result, some artists simplify their designs and substitute acrylic yarn to create pieces that can be sold for a greater profit to people who do not understand or value, quality and heritage.

Operating a backstrap loom

Enter Máximo Laura.

This is the world from which Máximo Laura emerged. He was taught to weave by his father, also a master Weaver when he was nine years old, and joined his family of accomplished weavers, where he remained as an apprentice until he was twenty. When he left his hometown of Ayacucho, he took with him his love of weaving, inquisitive mind, and deep pride in his Andean heritage.

As a young man in his 20s, Máximo sold his tapestries to pay for his studies in literature. However, his love of tapestry took over, and he devoted himself to his art. He is highly self educated and speaks knowledgeably about pointillism - a concept he uses in the blending of his colours- and numerous artists, movements and cultural periods throughout history that have influenced his work

His career was launched in the 1980s, when he began adding his vibrant colours and forms to the pre-Colombian heritage designs, and iconography, to make them more contemporary while still maintaining the spirit of the message. At that time, this was considered very avant-garde.

Máximo's passion and love for his culture and art transcend languages. His calm, gentle nature is magnetic and reveals a deeply spiritual being at peace with himself, and the world around him. This intrinsic strength comes alive in his designs, and to fruition on his looms.

Weaving into the 21st-century

Máximo turns to the technology and tools of today to express the voice of his ancient culture and explains, " the idea is to live in this time, because my responsibility is for my time and this society." His work is in great demand, so he established a workshop in Lima where he has 38+ looms as well as areas for his materials, design space and exhibitions. Craftspeople he has personally trained, handle the time-consuming technical aspects of production, but his work is by no means mass-produced. Each weaving is his personal one-of-a-kind design, and he closely supervises the entire process.

Computers are also vital part of his operations, both for communicating with the world beyond his studio and country, and for his designs. The tapestries start with a simple line drawing (cartoon) that Máximo then scans into Photoshop, where he adds colours and plans textural elements. In his early days, his designs began in the form of paintings, but today he finds Photoshop much faster, and more flexible.

The next step is to select and blend the yarn colours. Máximo has hundreds of colours of alpaca and cotton yarn -far more than his ancestors ever dreamed of. But to create the exact shades he needs, he borrows from the concept of pointillism and groups multiple colours of yarn to fool the eye into seeing tonality that could not exist otherwise.

Using knowledge of pointillism he has developed a method of weaving with up to 12 fine threads together as one. :

Creating a custom set of bundles, he starts with the darkest colour, where all 12 are the same dark colour. In the next bundle, one or two yarns of a slightly lighter colour are added and two of the darkest removed.

On the third grouping, two more of the slightly lighter colour are added, plus one or two in the next lightest colour in the series. The darkest yarns are removed, always keeping the same number of fine yarns in each bundle. And so on, until you have a line of bundles ranging from dark to light or one colour to another. The lengths of yarn are wound together ready for weaving and are called "butterflies".

In the studio's Colour Laboratory, new sets of butterflies are made up for each new tapestry, and the weaver has them laid out on shelves beside the loom.

Máximo, demonstrating how he achieves the ombré affect in his tapestries.

Once the colours and designs are finalised, the cartoons are drawn onto the warp, and the slow process of weaving begins. Here shapes are filled in and textural elements added, using supplementary wefts and a variety of stitches that Máximo has developed and is known for.

Máximo is committed to sharing his knowledge. He holds multiple conferences, symposiums and workshops, and he is passionate about inspiring young people. He has written a book about his art and also established a museum and library. The museum in Cusco houses his tapestries from the last 20 years, as well as the original paintings and cartoons from which they were produced. His collection of more than 1000 books will move to the library.

As Máximo himself says:

"My work is nourished by symbols, stories, traditions, rituals, experiences, and by permanently returning to admire the iconography of ancestral world cultures, especially Peruvian cultures. These experiences inspire me to discover, explore and absorb contemporary visual arts, which exist lavishly, choosing the one that moves me, and fits the direction of my visions of totem images, of symbolic characters and landscapes, and of my experience; developing ancestral patterns that are essentially Andean ".

Through Máximo Laura and others like him, the legacy of ancient Andean art and culture lives on.

www.maximolaura.com

Andean Symbolism
in Máximo's work

Throughout my career I have explored a number of themes and tapestry techniques but a constant has always been an ideal to create a continuity of Peru's textile history, to express my culture and tradition through a contemporary voice, combining a contemporary aesthetic with traditional techniques, designs, myths and symbols. Because of this, it is important to understand a number of Andean concepts when reading and understanding my tapestries.

The sun and the moon

In many of my tapestries you can find figures of the Sun or the Moon at the top of the piece. This is because in the Andean cosmology, the Inti or Sun God was one of the most important deities, the provider of warmth and light, a protector of the people.

According to legends, Inti taught his son and daughter the arts of civilization and they were sent to earth to pass this knowledge. The Sun still carries a very important role in the Andes today and there are many festivals and ceremonies celebrated around its importance, such as the Inti Raymi in the city of Cusco.

In other tapestries you can find a figure of the Moon instead of the Sun, which in Andean cosmology is Mama Killa, the Mother Moon and the sister of the Sun God. Traditionally, the Sun God is portrayed as a golden disk, while the Moon goddess is portrayed as a silver disk.

Complementary dualism

You might have seen tapestries where the Sun and Moon are shown together. This makes reference to the idea of Complementary Dualism found in Andean cosmology, understood as two opposite beings which are in need each other to create balance and stability. In this case, the dualistic relationship is between a Sun (male deity, the

Sun God) and the Moon (female deity, the Mother Moon). In this specific case, the dualistic view is also found in the cyclic way of viewing the world, such as the "fight" and complement of day and night, the sun and the moon, male and female.

In other tapestries you can see this concept represented by two faces displayed in opposite directions, but that might share a common characteristic such as an eye or the mouth.

This dualistic view of the world is found in many expressions of Andean cultures, from political and social organization, to religious ideas, rituals and creation myths. Dualism has many roots in pre-Columbian art, as we find zoomorphic creatures paired with inverted symmetries in the Andes as early as the Preceramic period. We can also find pairs and visual oppositions in most Andean cultures through time in silverwork, ceramic and architecture, but it is in woven textiles where we find this expression at its peak through anthropomorphized felines, birds, geometric patterns and designs.

The three realms

Another important concept found in my work comes from Andean cosmology, where the cosmos is divided in three realms or three pachas: Hanan Pacha, Kay Pacha and Uku Pacha. The three pachas represent different levels or existence that are interconnected by spiritual and mythical elements. They shaped the religion of the Incas and the life of the people.

The Hanan Pacha is the world of the above, of celestial beings, the world of the gods, of the Sun God and the Mother Moon. The Incas believed that one would ascend to the Hanan Pacha after death. This realm is traditionally represented by the figure of the condor, the Sun or the Moon and I also use the stars or flying beings as a representation of the Hanan Pacha.

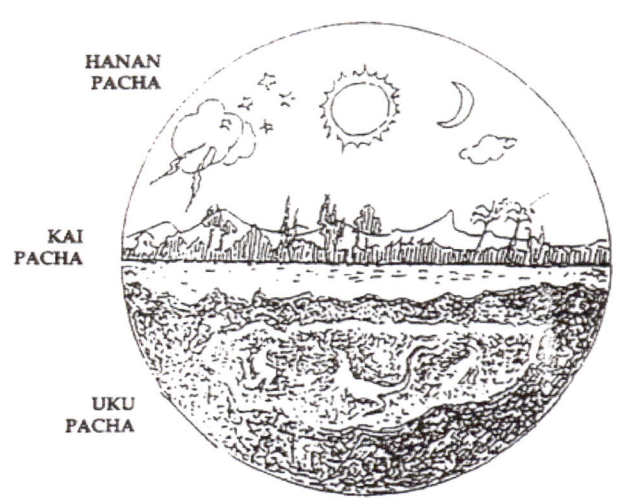

The sacred mountains or "Apus" are thought to have spirits that bridge the gap between man and the Hanan Pacha, which is why in the Andes many mountains and their peaks are viewed as sacred, and many times used as a location for ceremonies. This is why mountains are an important theme for many of my tapestries, sometimes found in the background of a tapestry or as the main theme of a piece.

The Kay Pacha is the middle world (literally meaning "this world"). This is the realm of the living, of the present, of humans, the earthly world. This realm is traditionally represented by the puma, although I also like to include jaguars or human figures to represent this realm.

The Uku Pacha is the inner world, the world of the dead as well as of the new life, the world of fertility, of earth and that which is beneath the earth. It is traditionally represented by a snake. In many of my works, I use different types of roots to symbolize this realm as well.

Now that you understand these three realms and their representations, you can see how I represent these same reals, in a visual way, through many of my tapestries. In many works you can find the Sun, the Moon, the stars or the Condor at the top of the design, representing the Hanan Pacha. In the middle you might be able to find human figures such as faces, or felines, representing the Kay Pacha. At the bottom of many tapestries you can find the figure of snakes or roots, representing the Uku Pacha.

With this information you can also understand the type of "arrow" figures that I add to some of my tapestries, going towards the top of the design, going from the earthly world (Kay Pacha) towards the upper world (Hanan Pacha) and creating a connection.

In the tapestry "Dwelling of the Condor", for example, you can see how the Moon and Sun are designed together, representing duality and the upper world. In the middle of the piece you can find several human faces (some are in the background of the design) representing middle world, and at the bottom of the piece you can see an icon (that you can also find in other tapestries) which looks like roots are alive, almost like a snake.

Inka cross

In some pieces you will also find the Inca Cross or "Chakana" which is one of the main symbols in the Andean world and has been found in a number of Andean cultures across history, from the Paracas, Chavin and Tiahuanaco Cultures, to the Incas.

A lot has been said about the meaning of the Chakana but it is believed that each of the three steps found on the corners of the Chakana is a representation of the three realms. The word "chakana" is thought to be born from the Quechua word "chaka" which means "bridge" or "union", and the suffix "-na" which means "instruments", so the Chakana is a symbol which represents an instrument of union between the 3 realms.

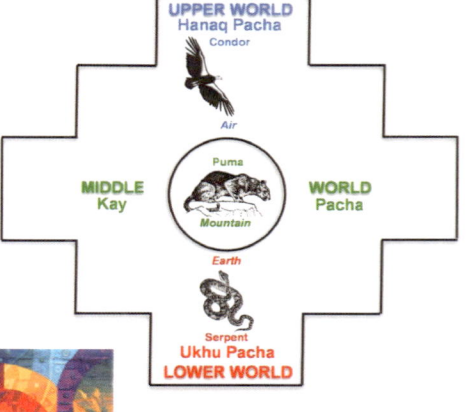

Musicians

We know through the account of the Spanish chronicles and through archeological evidence that music was an essential part of life in ancient Andean cultures. People played music in their homes for entertainment, but also as part of rituals. It was used in religious ceremonies such as burials, feasts and festivals, as well as in political activities. It was also used to heal the sick and to communicate with their ancestors. We can find evidence of this in wind instruments made from bone used in pre-Columbian ceremonies, and through its representation in ceramic, textiles and silver work.

Today, music still plays a very important role in Andean society, not only as entertainment, but also as a part of traditional ceremonies and festivities, being the guitar, the harp, the pan flute and the drum among the most important instruments. This is why I created an entire collection about musicians, some are playing together in the crop fields during harvest festivities, for example, while others are dancing traditional dances from the Andes.

Birds and sealife

Lastly, I have made a collection of tapestries about birds and sea life. I believe they carry a deeper meaning of peace and continuity of our natural landscape and planet in a time of global warming and pollution, in a time of crisis.

The collection about the sea life, is called the "Galapagos Collection", inspired by the incredible natural life found in the Galapagos Islands in Ecuador. Although I'm from the town of Ayacucho located in the Andes, I've lived more than 30 years in Lima, in the coast of Peru, with a close relationship with the ocean.

Patterns

You can also find patterns that repeat through many of my tapestries, so it is important to make a note about the meaning of these patterns or motifs.

CIRCLES:

Circles in the Andean cosmology carry a meaning of cycles, of cyclical time and transformation, a way to understand the world where cycles of time recur and events with them, so the circle motifs represent this cyclical time, especially when the theme of the piece is related to harvest or seasons. In a more physical representation, many tapestries have motifs that carry the shape of natural landscapes, sometimes seen from a bird´s eye view. This way we can see the circles in some tapestries are representations of lakes.

CHECKERED PATTERNS:

These patterns also represent a natural landscape, and in this case, they represent the crop fields in the Andes, when seen from a bird's eye view. It is interesting to find these three patterns when flying through the Andes, with this privileged view we are able to see the lakes as small circles, the crop fields as checkered patterns and, if seen from a low altitude, the Andean terraces.

ZIGZAG PATTERNS :

We find these patterns in several tapestries, as the circles, they also represent a natural landscape. These patterns represent Andean terraces, steps created in the Andean slopes that are still in use today to farm, created and used not only by the Incas but by a number of Pre-Inca cultures to work on very steep areas. The terraces have shaped the Andean landscape for thousands of years and you can still see them all across the landscape when traveling through Peru and other Andean countries.

Rosalind Johansson
a life in textiles

Born in London during the post-World War II years, my early memories are somewhat hazy. But by the age of about 5 the family had bid farewell to our multigenerational abode in Islington, North London, as my father secured the role as an assistant housing manager in the promising New Town of Welwyn Garden City. Subsequently we embarked on yet another move, this time to Hampshire. Amidst these transitions, my mother's determination to master her City and Guilds dressmaking examinations, filled our home with an array of fabrics and intriguing haberdashery.

In the midst of this creative whirlwind, I found myself captivated by the world of fabric and design. My parents, who wholeheartedly embraced creativity, encouraged my endeavours. Our adventures ranged from rustic camping in the garden, complete with wood-fire cooked meals (often somewhat charred), to donning imaginative ensembles, and staging impromptu plays. Even during holidays our paint boxes were ever-present companions.

However, even a story rooted in creativity can encounter detours. As I set my sights on attending Art College, an unexpected impediment came my way. My parents, influenced by the times, were hesitant about such aspirations, believing that only the unconventional attended art colleges. Furthermore, they echoed the sentiment that the creative sector lacked opportunities. Little did they know how mistaken that perspective was!

Navigating this crossroads, I eventually found a compromise that led me down an unexpected path with a role in the civil service as a map maker. Stationed in Whitehall, London. I underwent rigourous training in hand-drawn maps, and the intricate details required to update existing Ordinance Survey maps. The discipline required was demanding, yet it held a charm of its own.

After a three-year stint in London, I began to sense a heaviness creeping in. Seeking change, I decided to venture into the realm of volunteering, and I found the Steiner organisation. This unique group is dedicated to nurturing both children and adults with mental disabilities, helping them flourish and find joy in their lives. It was in this caring environment that I stumbled upon the world of handweaving for the very first time. It captured my imagination in an instant.

Fast forward a handful of years and my experiences at the Steiner schools had led me to train and work as a teacher in England. But, the winds of destiny blew and I decided to pack my bags and head to Sweden!

There in the midst of a new chapter, an extraordinary opportunity knocked on my door - the chance to immerse myself in the art of weaving. The course I found, conveniently located near my new home, had the exciting title of "Traditional Weaving and Embroidery". It was a full-time hands-on journey into the techniques that once wove the very fabric of Swedish culture when traditional home-crafted clothing was the norm.

Little did I know that this course would ignite a lifelong flame within me - a fervent passion for ethnic textiles, and the rich tapestry of traditional clothing. The journey didn't end with the conclusion of the course. I went home, inspired, and set up, not one but two floor looms. Armed with my trusty Husqvarna sewing machine. I embarked upon my creative endeavours, weaving fabrics and making cozy cushions and stylish bags out of Swedish wool.

In addition, inspired by a charming book penned by a Danish duo, Elsebeth Gynther and Bjarne Solberg, I found myself creating a variety of children's clothing using patchwork and quilting techniques for the first time. The pages of the book became a map, guiding me through new techniques in fabric, design and appliqué.

And so, from London's urban hustle to the Swedish forests, my journey unfolded, weaving together diverse experiences, and igniting a passion that would thread its way through my life.

Unfortunately, 1970s Sweden wasn't quite ready to embrace anything beyond its traditional styles and handicrafts, leaving my creations without much appeal or success in the market. Yet the wisdom gained from these endeavours would later prove invaluable during a new adventure in Africa.

Life has a funny way of circling back around. Six years later I found myself imparting my knowledge of weaving and sewing to a group of young and vulnerable women in Botswana. My role was facilitated through Norway's development programme, which specifically aimed to empower women by imparting practical skills

The job had its challenges. To begin with, the leading women in the organisation had migrated from South Africa in the 60s, fleeing apartheid.

Naturally, they met my arrival, (a white woman) with more than a hint of scepticism, but over time we forged a camaraderie that was both kind and supportive . As we tackled the challenges of our mission together, we met with countless adventures and shared much laughter. I will always remember them with respect and love. They taught me so much.

Whilst my bosses were responsible for overall management and recruitment, my responsibilities encompassed a wide range, from teaching to product design and quality control. Also day-to-day management of the workshop and finding sales outlets for our products. From a modest beginning of just four young women we soon became fourteen, including my wonderful Bellina, who was recruited to take over after me.

After four years, my contract was sadly over and I made my way back to the UK. There I became involved in the world of primary school education once again, focusing on special needs students and art and craft teaching.

The pull of Africa remained strong. After my nest was emptied on my children's departure, I felt a yearning to return to the continent. Tanzania beckoned this time with an opportunity at an International School nestled on the slopes of Mount Kilimanjaro.

I loved my job, the school, my colleagues, and our international group of students. How I would have loved to go to school like that myself!

The tale of my textile workshop there is one of serendipity. It began with a twist of fate as a Tanzanian colleague, a part-time art teacher, fell gravely ill with cerebral malaria.

His wife reached out, seeking a way to support the family while he battled his illness. She shared her lovely batiks, inspired by her husband's work, and asked if I could sell them for her. Before long, her artistic abilities found a home in my backyard.

At around the same time, a friend from the local hospital offered me a curious gift - used X-rays! The hospital was not happy about burning them when patients didn't take them home.

I saw potential. 'STENCILS'! I thought, and so our fabric printing workshop took its first breath. Armed with my newly cut stencils and some fabric paint, the local ladies adorned locally bought cotton with vibrant printed patterns. Yes, you read that right - ladies in the plural! The story was just beginning and the cast of characters was growing.

Before I knew it, other young women facing their own challenges were knocking on our workshop door, seeking a chance at employment. Over time our ranks swelled to four, two deftly working the printing table and two more handling the sewing tasks.

How did I juggle two roles you might ask? Well one delightful perk was the lack of a commute. No daily rush-hour to fight through. But the real secret lay in timing.

The school day started bright and early at 7:30 am, which meant that we also finished early in the afternoon, barring any meetings, parent conferences or preparation work. Once school obligations were met, I strolled home across the playing fields. My industrious team awaited me. They would fill me in on the days happenings and I would dive into preparing activities for the upcoming day.

Stencilled African Pots and Baskets

We found a handsome model for our hand-printed shirts

My to-do list could encompass a bit of teaching, quality checks, product design, stencil cutting, colour mixing and researching sales outlets for our creations. It was like déja vu from my Botswana days, and it warmed my heart to watch my little team blossom with newfound confidence and skills.

All good things come to an end, and after a rewarding stretch of nearly 8 years, I bid farewell to Tanzania and set my compass for the UK. I wanted to be near my aging parents as they were becoming frail. Yet my love affair with Patchwork and Quilting was just beginning. I had to fit it in between part time teaching jobs and I was on a mission to delve into this world of colour, fabric and pattern. Determination fuelled me, I was determined to become successful in this field, soaking up every bit of knowledge I could lay my hands on.

'Heavy Burdens', one of my first Africa quilts using kitenge fabric and stencilled panels from our workshop

One of the challenges was how to use my African fabrics in patchwork and quilting. Beautiful as they are, they posed quite a puzzle. After much contemplation and experimentation, I came up with a solution. Armed with boxes upon boxes of African fabric, especially 'KITENGE' which I had lugged back from Tanzania (Yes I'm slightly obsessed). I embarked on a mission to create African inspired quilts. To blend these fabrics attractively, I combined them with my hand-dyed fabrics and even incorporated stencil panels from our workshop's artistic production.

Eventually, I started to take part in quilt and textiles shows across the UK. I found myself exhibiting at prestigious events like The Festival of Quilts in Birmingham, Quilts UK, and the Knitting and Stitching Shows in London and Harrogate and many more. I also led workshops and guided fellow quilters on Textile Tours to exciting destinations, like Tanzania and Sweden. Additionally, I had the opportunity to teach Africa-themed days in schools all over the country. These sessions involved exploring traditional East African clothing, particularly the unique design elements of the Kanga. The children even block-printed their own, to cap off the day we would finish with a rousing song in Swahili.

And so, from the discipline of a weaving course, in Sweden, to the heart of Africa's creative spirit, my journey unfolded, intertwining threads of diverse experiences, and a steadfast passion for textiles.

In 2015, I decided to visit Peru, having long wished to explore the heritage of textiles and design there. I signed up for a Textile Tour and accompanied by a friend, embarked on the lengthy journey from London to Lima. It was during our initial days in the city, that we had a chance to visit Máximo Laura's studio.

It's funny how appearances can be so deceiving. The unassuming street we stepped into hid an unexpected trove of treasures, waiting to be discovered!

Little did I know I was about to be completely captivated by the vibrant palette, the multiple textures, the intricate symbols, the artistic designs, and the enchanting play of light in Máximo's tapestries! It was an immediate and immersive experience that blew my mind.

This marked the beginning of my extended trips to Peru, where I studied Spanish and ventured into the heart of the southern landscape, exploring the domains of craftsmen and artists. But Máximo's work kept tugging me back, a call I couldn't resist, which led me to enroll in a workshop at his Lima studio - an immersive experience, shared by five fortunate souls, including myself. Under the tutelage of Máximo himself, and two master weavers, we embarked on a whirlwind three week journey, aiming to complete our square metre masterpiece within this time span.

Máximo had readied a palette of simpler designs for us to choose from. With a twinkle in his eye, he promised to teach us at least twelve of the 30+ textural stitches that he weaves into his creations. The work was hard, carried out on uncomfortable floor looms, but the presence of our shelves full of colourful 'butterflies' and the gradual unfolding of our woven pieces maintained our focus. The days were interspersed with delicious meals, created by Máximo's gracious wife; moments of sustenance, conversation and enjoyment punctuated intense work sessions.

Máximo teaching me at the Loom

Surrounded by Máximo's handiwork, an electrifying spark ignited within me, a curious thought began to swirl around my brain. Could these designs find a home in the world of quilting? The journey would entail finding the right balance - adapting one of the less intricate designs and capturing the characteristic ombré. Ombré is where colours seamlessly transition from light to dark, or from one hue to another. But where would one find such fabric? Could such materials even be procured or would I need to take the dyeing and painting route? More importantly, what would Máximo think about such a strange idea? .

My delight as my woven tapestry comes off the loom and I see it whole for the first time

With my heart racing I posed the question to Máximo. Would it be possible to borrow one of his designs to translate into a quilt? He was intrigued. Quilting was something that he had not yet encountered. Nevertheless, he graciously granted his consent.

And so I embarked on the journey of quilting some of Máximo's designs, weaving stitches of cloth, instead of thread, interpreting the design in a new way and exploring the potential of machine quilting to give texture. It was a puzzle to solve , a challenge to embrace, uncovering methods that harmonised the tapestry inspired designs with a quilt making art form.

One serendipitous evening, as conversation flowed over beers and camaraderie, a single word set a spark ablaze. BOOK! The idea kindled curiosity and much discussion. Soon it was unanimous. I would make several quilts and discuss the project with Máximo.

And now, after several years in the making, somewhat derailed by the pandemic's unwelcome intervention, the result stands before you. It's a fusion of Máximo's artistry, a desire to share it with a wider audience, and my unrelenting compulsion to translate it into an alternative form, a tribute to his brilliance, woven into the fabric of my life, seeking to resonate with those who appreciate beauty born from tradition, innovation, and a shared passion for creative expression.

www.spiritofcreativity.co.uk

Materials, Fabrics and Haberdashery

I thought a brief overview of materials might be of use.

Fabrics

Firstly we need to think about fabrics.

They are the building blocks of our creative canvas and ombré fabrics are, without doubt the most useful when emulating Máximo Laura's designs. They have the ability to capture the changing light and shifting shades that you will find in the tapestries.

But they can also be frustrating when the transition from one shade or colour to another is too slow. Make your quilts larger, rather than smaller and you will find this less of a problem.

Ombré fabrics are not very common, although some with spots and stars have made a comeback recently. Here are some that I use :

Caryl Bryer Fallert has two ranges which she used extensively in her superb quilts They are called Graduations and Essentials, distributed by Benartex and they are a very reliable choice. Their vivid hues channel the spirit of Máximo's designs wonderfully.

British designers, Lewis and Irene, offer a small array of eye-catching ombré fabrics that might also fit the bill.

Jennifer Sampou has designed an extensive Sky Fabric range for Robert Kaufmann. They originated as soft, pastel paintings, and the fabrics encompass a wide spectrum of colour from bold to understated offering an alternative to the Benartex range.

Alternatively, hand-dyed fabrics, your own or purchased, can add texture and you will find blenders and other prints which work.

If you haven't come across them, Mickey Lawler's Skydyes and Skyquilts books can guide you through the journey of painting your own fabrics.

Lastly, batiks can be useful too. Their tightly woven nature comes in handy for raw-edge appliqué, resisting fraying, and adding stability.

Wadding/Batting

Other essentials, are of course, wadding or batting. This inner layer is the backbone of every quilt, offering warmth and structure. Again the options are quite diverse. -

When it comes to these particular quilts, a high-loft polyester wadding might not be your best bet. However, if you like working with it, try it out and see how it performs.

As for my personal preference. I like a medium-loft cotton and polyester blend typically a 60/40% mix. Some versions come with a very thin muslin backing. This might go well with my step-by-step techniques. Polyester and cotton blends tend to be cooperative and give a pleasing texture when machine quilted.

Freezer Paper

As the name implies, freezer paper was originally designed for storing food in the freezer, but has proved to be very useful in quilt making. It's a semi-transparent, greaseproof paper that features a delicate plastic layer on one side and it's very versatile.

You can trace your pattern pieces onto freezer paper, cut them out and then firmly iron them onto the fabric's right side. Once you've cut the fabric to shape and neatly tacked it into place, the freezer paper pattern or template can be peeled off carefully and leaves no sticky residue. You can reuse the same piece multiple times, which is useful with recurring shapes.

Fusible Web

This product has several names, depending on the manufacturer. Vlieseline, Vliesofix, Wonder Under, Bondaweb and Iron-on adhesive.

It too is a grease-proof paper , but with a thin web of heat activated glue on one side. If you are not familiar with it, it enables you to cut shapes in your fabric and literally glue them in place. You trace your design onto the paper side. Placing the glue side down (very important) iron it onto the **reverse** of your fabric. You will need to reverse your design before tracing it, if the orientation is important. Otherwise it will be back to front.

Threads

Last but not least, threads. We all have our favourite go-to threads.

When considering making a "Máximo" quilt you will need to think about threads for tacking; threads for construction; threads for quilting and if you opt for some satin stitch, to emphasise important design lines in the quilt, or other decorative stitching, you will need suitable weights and colours for that too.

I won't tell you what threads to use as what is available depends on which continent you live.

It's a good idea to make up some small quilt sandwiches to test the threads i.e. what weight of thread, what type of needle you are thinking of using. If you use the fabric you will be using in the quilt you can test the colours as well.

The thread colour is important. You can change the apparent colour of the fabric if you quilt with a contrasting thread and "knock back" areas that are too bright. You can even quilt in an "ombré" fashion, gradually changing the colour of the quilting if your fabric doesn't do that for you. "Micro stippling" can completely change or block out the colour of the fabric and affect the value.

'The Beloved', my finished version.

Step by Step
Project 1: The Beloved

This design is part of a larger tapestry. I took it together with part of a second tapestry to create a diptych. You can see both the original tapestries as well as my quilted diptych in the Gallery section.

There are many methods to make a quilt. To make Máximo's tapestry designs, I have often used an unconventional one. I have mounted the pieces directly onto the wadding. The pieces feel too fragile to sew together in the normal way, and the wadding doesn't stretch or pull out of shape .

Alternatively, one could use a plain cotton fabric, tacking the pieces in place in the same way if working with wadding doesn't appeal to you. Or, of course, you could sew the pieces together as you go along in the normal way.

The choice is yours

Here is my method of working.

Part of Máximo's tapestry

Preparation

Print or photocopy the line printout (cartoon), the size you want your finished quilt to be. Use a lightbox or a convenient window to make two tracings. One tracing should be on freezer paper and you will use this as your pattern.

The second one is on tracing paper. This is to use as an overlay to check positioning, especially towards the completion of the work when the freezer paper pattern pieces are cut up.

The two tracings

Design for the Quilt. Enlarge to your desired size.

Cut a piece of wadding (or plain fabric, if you choose that alternative), the size of your finished quilt +2 inches or 5 cm all round. Place the freezer paper onto it and run a tacking thread all around to mark the edge. .

It can be helpful to number the pieces(I numbered mine from the centre outwards, see diagram). Also I marked the pattern so that later I can line up the marks when positioning pattern pieces.

Gather your fabrics. A selection of ombré fabrics and one or two others(for the hair) for example.

Have a colour photocopy or the photograph from this book of Máximo's tapestry to refer to when choosing the colours.

Now you are ready to start.

A selection of mostly ombré fabrics

Method

Starting in the middle, cut out the face pattern. Select the fabric and iron the freezer paper on top of it. Cut out the fabric, leaving a quarter inch border all round the pattern.

 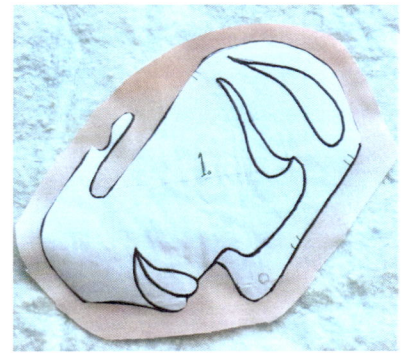 

Pattern and face fabric pinned exactly in place. Tack round carefully

Replace the freezer paper patern, lining it up exactly with your tacking. Pin it securely in place and then insert the face pattern and fabric into hole lining up any markings exactly. Tack round the face carefully, right against the edge of the pattern. It's very important to have this first piece exactly in the right place.

Add the next piece, the neck and shoulder, and after tacking, carefully peel off the freezer paper.

I will now add piece 3, as the leaves should be added later. It's important to work out from the centre.

Next prepare the fabric for the hair.

Piece 3 pinned in place

Iron the pattern onto the hair and cut out. Note which sides are cut exactly(to go over an underlap) and which sides need a quarter inch border to become an underlap later. Make sure at least two sides have an under lap or you could end up with a space where fabrics don't meet.

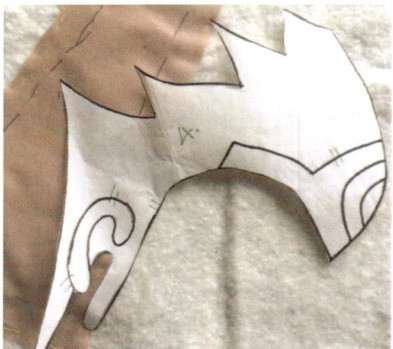

Cut out the pattern for the hair, piece 4

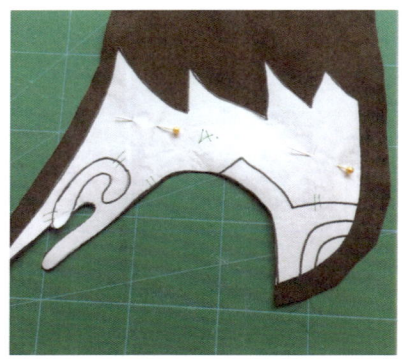

Piece 4 ironed to fabric

Place the fabric and pattern into place and tack down to secure. The face has now been surrounded by pattern pieces and we start working outwards.

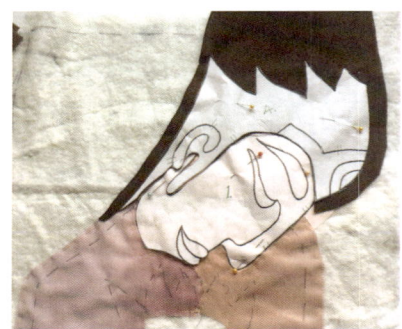

Hair fabric now pinned in place ready for tacking

Next prepare piece 5. This goes at the back of the head and will later have decorative strips added.

First select ombré fabric referring to colour picture. Iron on the pattern piece.

Select ombré fabric for piece 5

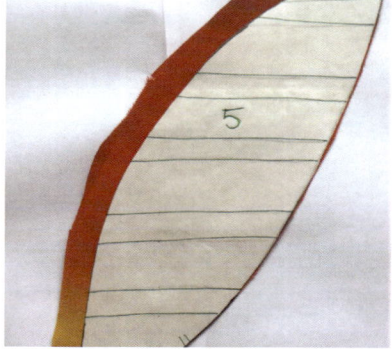

Freezer paper ironed on

Pin in position and then tack

After pinning in position check using overlay and then tack securely. Note in the illustration how the tacking on the hair is very careful so that placements of adjoining pieces will be accurate.

Continue adding pieces in the same way and build up the background construction of the quilt.

You will need to "fussy cut" your fabrics in order to achieve the colour graduations required. It seems a bit wasteful but scraps can be used later.

Add the band tacking securely in position.

More pieces added

The long band tacked in place

Now add many of the smaller parts which go on top of existing pieces. Ear, eyebrow, headdress and foliage can all be put in place. These pieces have had bondaweb(or similar) ironed on the back, so they can be fused in place before sewing.

Working on the right hand side

Main piece in place and tacked down

The main construction is now complete.

Now, some of the decorative elements can be added.

Select the fabrics and iron bondaweb to the back before cutting out. Remove the paper backing, position carefully and iron into place.

Where possible tuck any ends into the underlap. Where this isn't possible, trim off neatly.

Iron bondaweb to the back of your fabric before cutting out the shapes

Some of the decorative pieces ironed in place

Trim where necessary. Carefully cut face pattern to mark details of the nose and eye

Now replace the freezer paper pattern and cut carefully round the nose and eye to enable markings to be transferred.

Markings for nose and eye transferred

Mark through the gap carefully.

Using a machine satin stitch at your desired width, sew the markings for the nose and eye. Then continue sewing all the major pieces with a wide satin stitch and sewing down smaller elements with a normal straight stitch.

Satin stitch around all the shapes

Use fabric pencils or paint to add depth to the face.

Decide about your backing and binding. I used the bagging out method (put backing right side down on quilt, stitch round using quarter inch seam and leave hand sized space at base to turn quilt through. Turn quilt through, push out corners and iron edges. Sew the gap by hand.)

Quilt as desired.

Add hanging sleeve and label.

Alternatively, add backing and binding using your favourite method.

Quilt 'bagged out'

Step by Step
Project 2: Conciliation

"Conciliation" by Máximo Laura

Preparation

This beautiful design has been named Conciliation by Máximo. Central are the two birds holding out olive branches of peace.

It's a very complex design and needs more than one technique to put it together. Whatever techniques you decide to use, here are some hints on preparation.

Requirements for this quilt

Ombré fabrics such as Graduations and Essentials by Caryl Bryher Fallert for Benartex, Sky Fabrics by Jennifer Sampou, ombré by Lewis and Irene or hand dyed/painted fabrics you have sourced or produced yourself.

Wadding/batting (high loft polyester is not recommended) I prefer a medium loft cotton/polyester blend.

A backing fabric.

A selection of suitable coloured threads

Your favourite quilt making tools.

Ombré fabrics. Graduations and Essentials by Benartex.

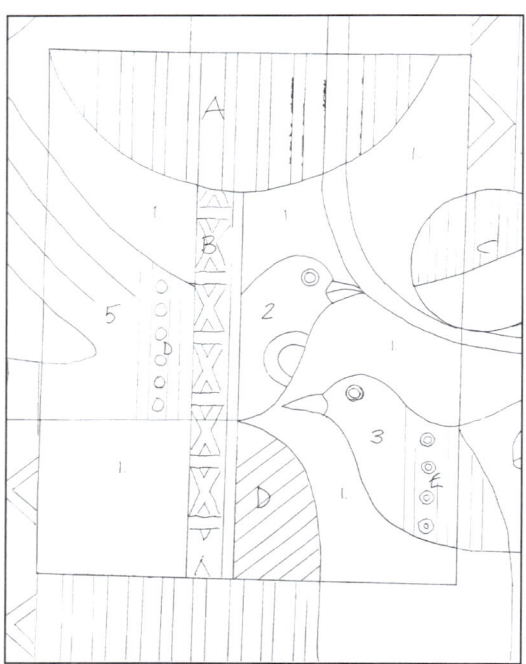

Lineart (cartoon). Find it in the Design Templates chapter

1. The line print-out needs to be photo-copied or printed out to your desired size.

   Mine here is 23"x26.5". (58.5cms x 67.5cms).

2. Using a light table or a convenient window trace off a copy onto freezer paper.

   Trace off a further line copy onto tracing paper. This will help you check your placements.

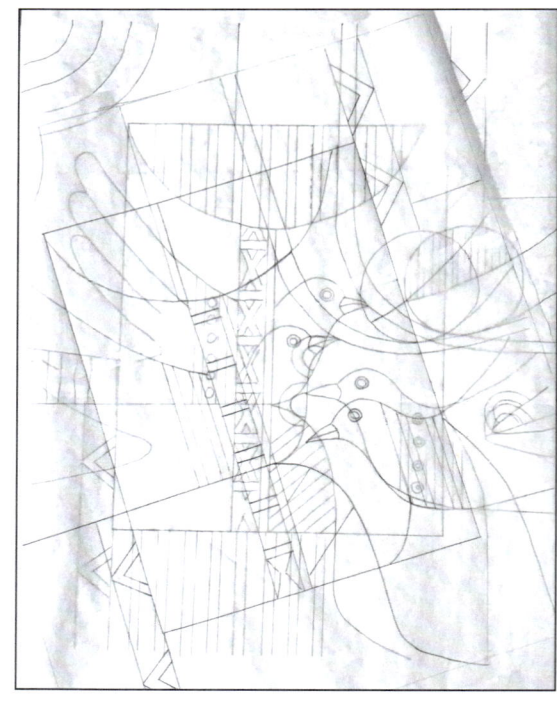

Freezer paper tracing with tracing paper overlay on top.

If you are using Máximo's colour palette, you will also need an A3 or A4 size photocopy of the original tapestry., as above.

Cut out the wadding/batting, making sure that it's at least 2 inches or 5 centimetres larger than the finished size of your quilt.

There are several ways one could approach making this quilt. I have chosen to mount the raw edge appliqué on the wadding, adding the backing later. That's the method I'm going to illustrate here.

Method, section one

1. I've decided to work on the central rectangle, basically yellow, separately from the outer frame, basically blue, although the two overlap here and there.

2. I'm going to work on the more complex elements as separate pieces and put them together afterwards. For example, the large semicircle and the ladder design. They are labelled A B C etc. they can be machine pieced or appliquéd.

3. The other pieces, labelled 1, 2, 3, etc will be fussy cut and appliquéd onto the yellow background.

4. Label your pieces on the freezer paper copy. Do not cut them out at this stage. Label the sections.

 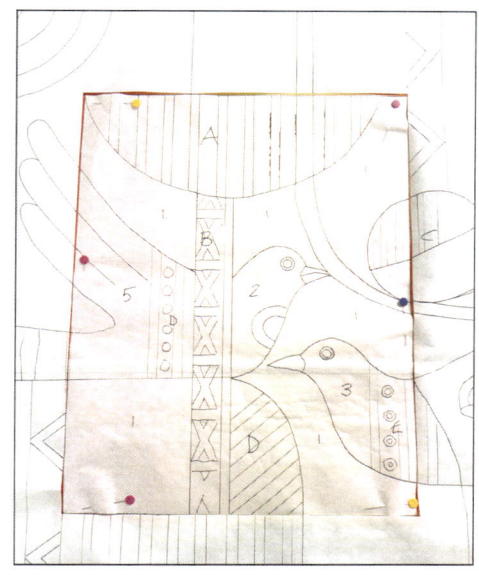

5. Cut out the central section of the freezer paper, the central rectangle.

6. Iron the freezer paper to the yellow/red ombré fabric.

7. Cut this out, leaving a quarter inch border all round.

8. Place the rectangle of freezer paper and fabric back in the hole, matching it exactly. Now tack all the way round in the tiny gap between the central rectangle and the frame. This puts the yellow rectangle exactly in place and the tacking stitches will show exactly where the blue frame pieces will be placed later.

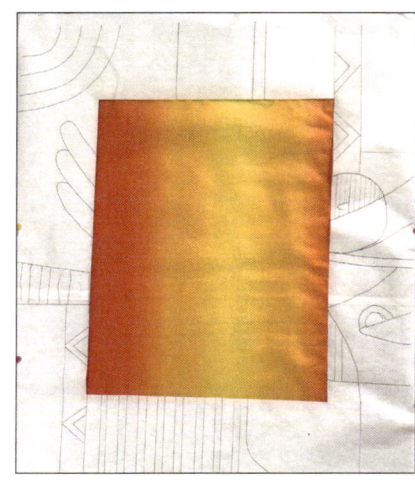

Remove the freezer paper. Lay the wadding and freezer paper with the fabric rectangle to one side.

Method section two: Elements

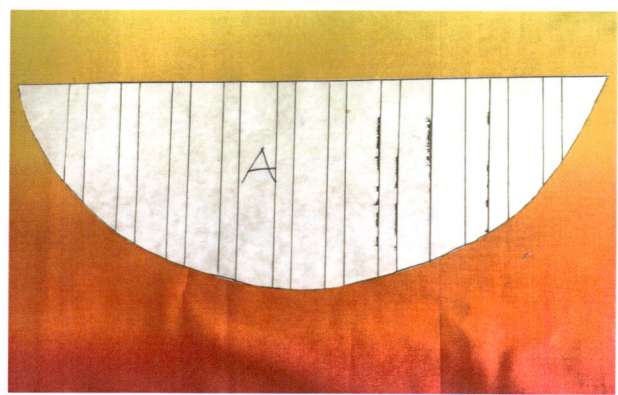

Shape A ironed to yellow/red ombré fabric

1. The large semicircle. This could be pieced but here I show how to appliqué it.

2. Cut out shape A and iron it onto your ombré fabric.

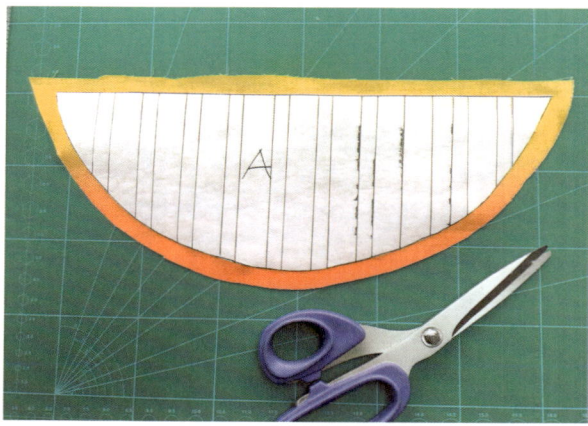

3. Cut out leaving a quarter inch border all round.

4. Cut out a rectangle of dark blue ombré for the stripes. Iron bondaweb to the back. It will help reduce fraying.

Iron bondaweb to blue ombré fabric

5. Cut a rectangle of dark blue

6. Cut 9 strips. The width will depend on what size you are working with. Measure on the print-out. Remove bondaweb backing.

Cut strips that run across from dark to light

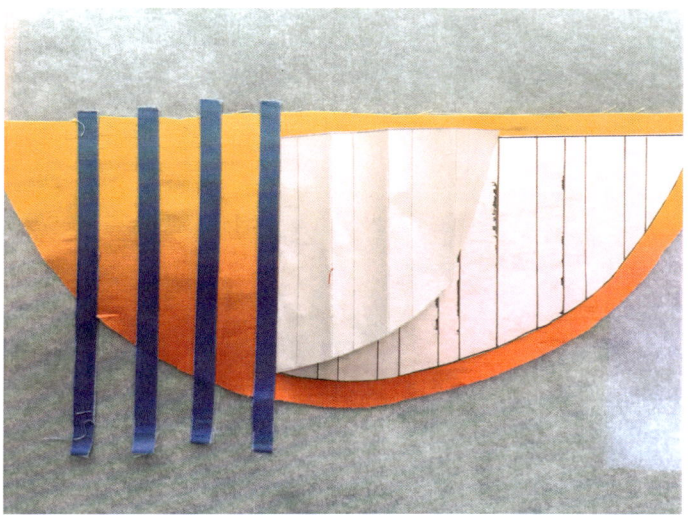

By carefully folding back the freezer paper you can accurately place the strips

7. Use FP to position strips. Iron down. Cut the purple/blue wider strip and fuse in place. Strips all fused in place. You can leave the element A as is or face it to give a firmer neater edge. Facing added.

(FP=Freezer Paper)

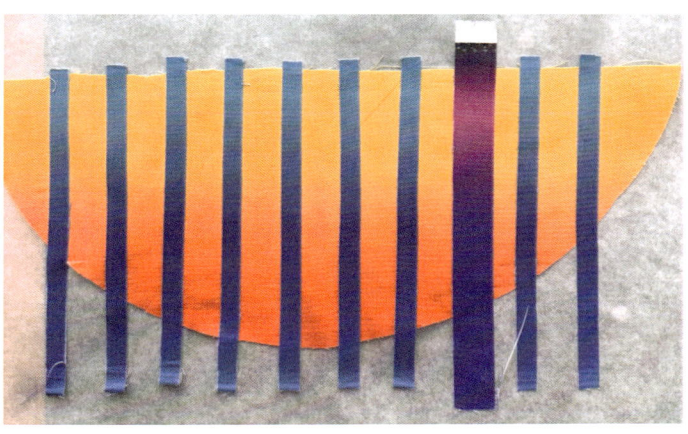

Iron down the strips

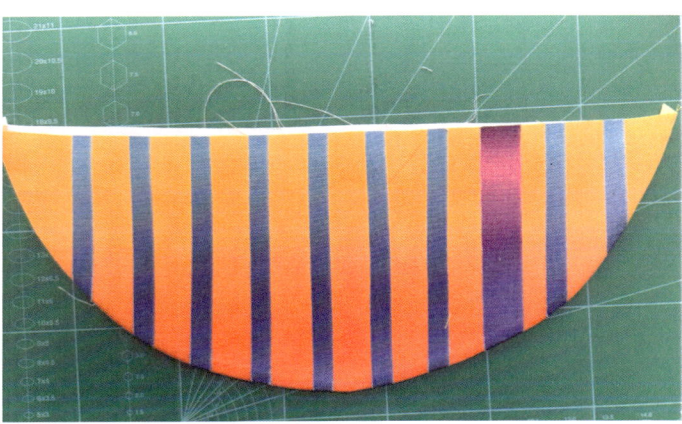

Optional facing

Next the "ladder", shape B.

8. First make the background strip, piecing fabrics as necessary background strip with FP.

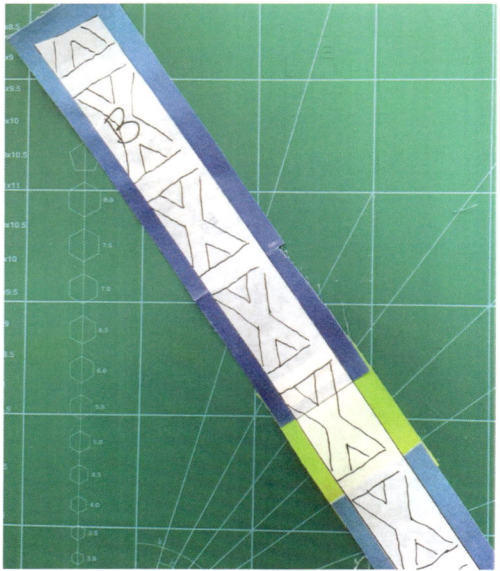

Fabric background to 'ladder' section with FP ironed on top

9. Carefully trace the crosses onto bondaweb and iron to the back of your chosen fabrics. Cut out the crosses. cut out and fuse in place.

Crosses have bondaweb on back. Peel back the FP to get placement

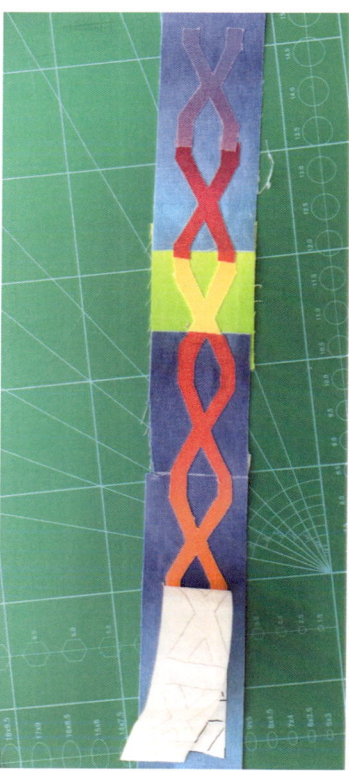

Crosses ironed in place

10. Assemble the crosses. By peeling back a section of freezer paper at a time you can ensure each cross is in the correct position before fusing in place. Fuse using FP to aid placement.

11. Cut out the cross bars (backed with bondaweb) and iron down. Iron crossbars in place.

12. Measure and cut the strip to the left of the ladder. You will have to sew 2 together a achieve the abrupt colour change which continues across the ladder and level with the bottom edge of the bird's breast.

Shape D

You could cut repeat narrow strips or settle for 3 as here

Choosing fabric for shape D

13. Depending on your fabric choice, piece or appliqué this to achieve the ombré effect. Facing gives a clean sharp edge.

I decided to face this shape

Shape C

14. This shape overlaps onto the blue frame of the quilt design but I would advise making it as one piece. Add strips where indicated and use the freezer paper templates to sew the pieces together accurately. Use FP.

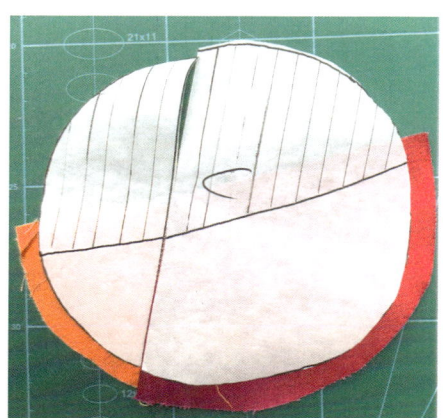

Ready to add the striped section

15. Sewing the sections together.

Now using the Freezer paper as a guide, position all the shapes in their correct places.

Band sewn to ladder and shapes tried out in position

Method, section three: Birds

Select fabric for birds.

1. Iron freezer paper onto bird fabric and cut out. Make sure there is a quarter inch under lap on each bird where it will join the rest of its body.

Freezer paper and bondaweb preparation

Pieces ironed in place

2. Trace all the small pieces, eyes, beaks and decorative elements onto bondaweb. Iron to back of chosen fabric scraps and cut out.
3. Iron the small pieces in place.

4. Both birds ready.

5. Stitch the details on the birds. Cut out the freezer paper labelled 6, a long strip, and iron to the fabric. Cut this on the line but allow a quarter inch under lap each end. Time to sew details on the elements if you haven't done so earlier. They are easier to sew before assembly.

Birds placed and strip 6 cut and placed

Everything placed, pieces placed ready for sewing

Tip: If you would like the stitching to be more obvious, use an 80 sized needle and put 2 normal weight threads in the top or one heavier thread. The advantage with 2 is they don't have to be the same colour. For example, pink with maroon gives a nice effect, like wise, blue and turquoise.

Finish the elements and shapes and place and iron down, using the freezer paper as a guide. When happy everything is where it should be, sew it in place.

Sewing completed

Method section four: the blue frame

Pin the freezer paper frame back in position

1. Replace the freezer paper frame and pin in place.

2. Starting at the top left hand corner, cut out one piece of freezer paper at a time, select fabric and iron onto fabric. position and tack in place.

3. NB. Make sure you leave an under lap and use the line of tacking to show where the next piece will lie. Working left to right, decide which side the underlap will be. Without it you risk having a gap.

Top LH corner. Freezer paper and cut edge with underlap

4. The corner piece had to be cut in two to get the colours right. Here you can see how I joined it and worked under the overlapping bird tail.

Freezer paper removed. Piece tacked in place

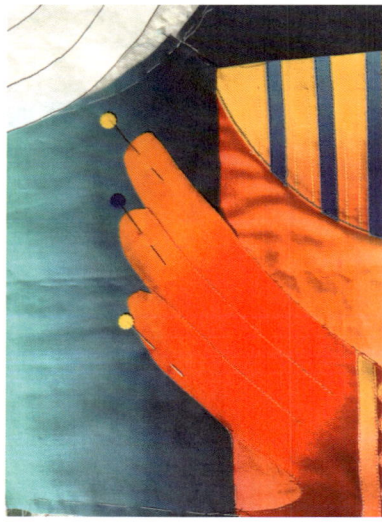

Tail feathers in place on top of background

5. Work along the top towards the right adding pieces and tacking in place.

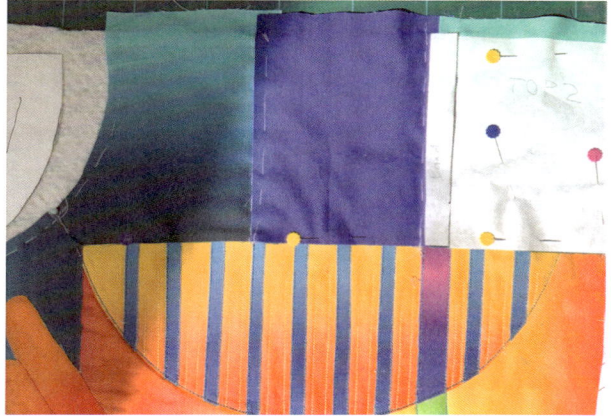 

Work along the top towards the right

6. top right hand corner.

Band and decorative strip added

7. Here you will need to deal with the band and the strip with decoration separately and then add them.

8. Corner pieces are added next.

   Tack them in place and keep replacing the freezer paper or using the tracing paper image to check the placement every time.

Corner pieces are added next

8 cont. There are several complex pieces to add down the right hand side.

Use the freezer paper as a pattern and refer to your picture of the tapestry to match the colours. Make sure to add underlaps when cutting out. It's better to have more than necessary than not!

The pieces to the right of the circle and under it, are now in place. Pin and tack down.

9. The next group of pieces needs to be put together first before placing. First iron the freezer paper pattern pieces to the fabric. Check the colours against Máximo's tapestry if you are using this colourway.

Use the freezer paper patterns and iron on fabric

10. You could piece this area if you wished. I fused it.

The complex area is now in position. Again check for accuracy with the traced overlay.

Right hand side now tacked in place

Bottom right hand corner.

11. Select the fabric. Iron on the freezer paper. Cut out and tack in place.

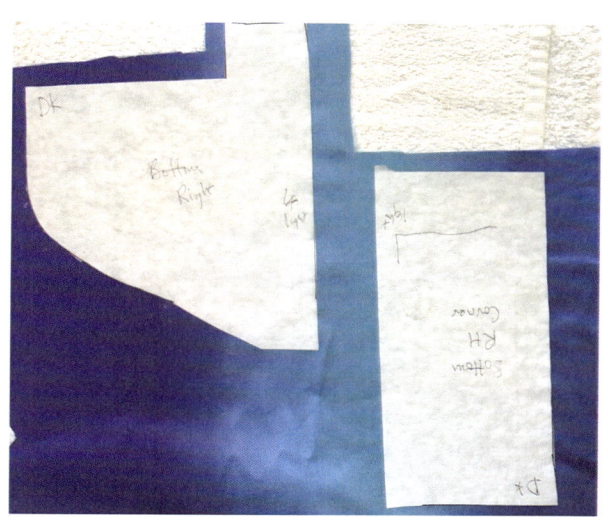

Tack the two pieces in place and peel off the freezer paper

12. Select, cut, place and sew the last corner piece.

Method, section five: completing the frame

The next section is another bank of stripes.

1. Cut out the back ground fabric and then iron bondaweb to the back of your stripe fabrics, noting the different colours. There are 3 dark, one light and 3 mixed.

2. Use the freezer paper to aid placing again and iron in place.
3. Tack the completed piece in place.

On to the bottom left hand corner.

4. This contains a decorative bar similar to the one made for the top right hand corner and another ombré fabric. Proceed as before and tack your pieces in place, checking with the traced overlay.

The bottom left hand corner with the decorative bar and ombré fabric tackd in place

Now all that remains of the basic construction is the tail of the bird with stripes and the concentric circles in the upper left hand corner.

6. Proceed in the same way as before to construct the striped tail of the bird and select and cut the fabrics for the concentric circle feature, upper left. When these are tacked in place, the whole of the wadding is covered and the main construction is complete.

Basic sewing completed, loose ends hidden and visible tacking threads removed

7. With all the pieces in place your quilt is ready for sewing!

8. Hide all the loose ends inside or neatly on the back and remove the visible tacking threads as you go.

See my completed quilt, including the all important olive branches in the bird's beaks on page 64.

Method, section six, completing the quilt

You now have a lot of decisions to make about how to finish your quilt.

Firstly, the backing.

Are you going to put the backing on now with a binding and use all the decorative stitching/details as the quilting?

Maybe you have already put the backing on because that's how you like to work.

Or are you going to "bag it out", having the quilt go to the very edge with no binding?

This is what I have chosen to do here but other quilts I have made with Máximo designs have bindings. You will find them in the Gallery.

Or do you want to frame the quilt with a border and a binding?

The choice is yours.

Secondly, the decorative stitching all over the quilt.

There are any number of ways you may want to interpret this, and if indeed you intend to include it at all.

Depending on the size of your quilt, you may decide it has enough detail and stands as it is, with basic quilting, such as stitch in the ditch or satin stitch to emphasise some of the dominant lines within the composition.

Or, you may decide to fuse some of the circles and triangles in place and machine stitch them down.

Then there are the long, curly fronds, they could be hand embroidered or machine stitched.

And lastly, what about the areas where your ombré fabrics have just not changed colour fast enough or with the right colour graduations?

You could leave it as it is, or you could use fabric inks or paints to adjust it more to your liking.

All these choices are yours to make.

Included here are some photographs of my decisions on how to finish my version of "Conciliation".

I fused down the circles and rings and machine stitched them with a double thread to give a strong outline. I then did the same with the ombré triangles in the bottom right section.

I then hand embroidered the curly fronds. After that I trimmed and squared up the quilt and added the backing, using the bagging out method.

After pressing and hand sewing the opening at the bottom, I started to use my Inktense Sticks to adjust the colour in some areas. I wasn't happy with the dry effect so carefully tried adding a little water with a small brush. This worked better.

I then added a wide satin stitch to emphasise some main design shapes. Finally, I added some quilting in areas where I thought it needed.

Finally make your hanging sleeve and sew in place and add a label, always crediting Máximo Laura as the designer.

The "bagged out" quilt with decoration

Gallery

All tapestries in the gallery are by Máximo Laura. All quilts are made by Rosalind Johansson using Máximo's designs.

Abundant Fruit of the Sea - Tapestry 47" x 94"

Sun Temple on Equinox - Tapestry

These two tapestries are interesting because whilst using the same line-art (cartoon), the alternate colourways along with the addition of Andean symbolism create two totally different pieces.

Black Sun in the Intihuatana - Tapestry 47" x 78"

Fertility Cycle II - Tapestry 47" x 47"

*Vitalidad Marina
- Tapestry 47" x 68"*

Song of the Heart
- Tapestry 31" x 78"

Abundant Harvest Myth - Tapestry 47" x 47"

Harvest in the Field - Tapestry 23" x 49"

Jaguar Looking Towards the Sun - Tapestry 23" x 39"

Earth's Fire II - Tapestry 47" x 59"

Sowing in the Andean Sunset - Tapestry 47" x 31"

Birds on the Harvest Field - Tapestry 47" x 47"

Conciliation - Quilt 28" x 23"

Flight of Birds on the Field - Quilt 37" x 33"

Chant for Development - Quilt 46" x 34"

*This quilt is named by Máximo 'Sanctuario del Sol'
but I have renamed my version 'Voice of the Indigenous People' - Quilt*

Greater Spirit - Tapestry 47" x 47"

Offering to the Sun God - Tapestry 47" x 31"

Maximo's name for this design is Spirit of the Jaguar II but when I quilted it I interpreted it a different way and renamed it Total Eclipse - Quilt 47" x 31"

Moonlight - Quilt 47" x 31"

Warriors of Light - Tapestry 47" x 62"

Four Birds Towards the Sun - Tapestry

These two small quilts are designed to hang side by side. They are small parts of two larger tapestries (shown below).

Diptych 'The Beloved" - Quilts 47" x 31"

El Abrazo de la Amada - Tapestry 63" x 47"

Nostalgias de la Amada - Tapestry 70" x 47"

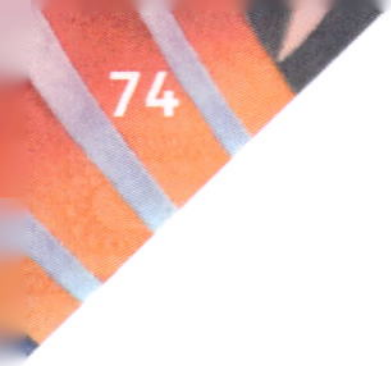

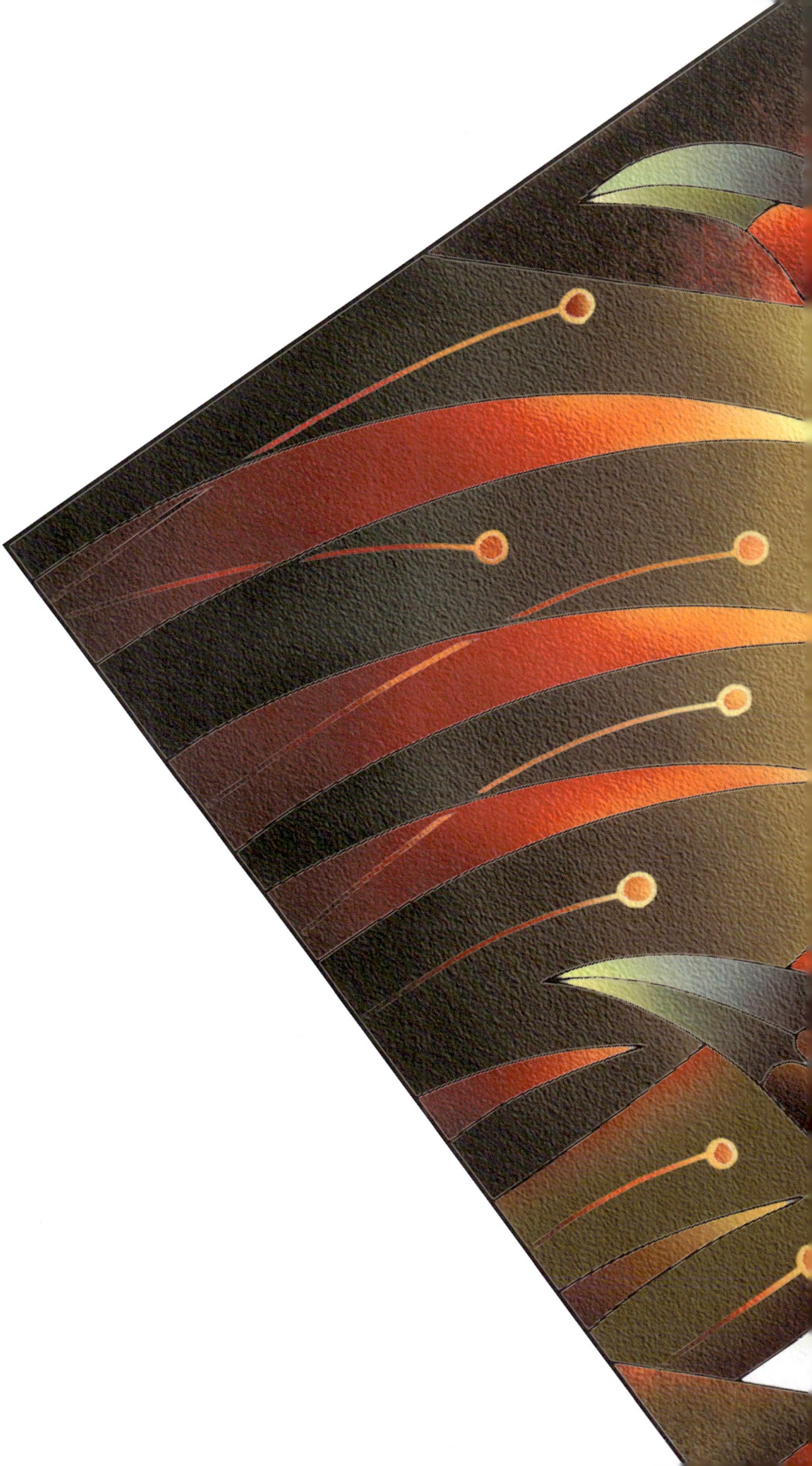

Design Templates

Conciliation - Tapestry 47" x 39"

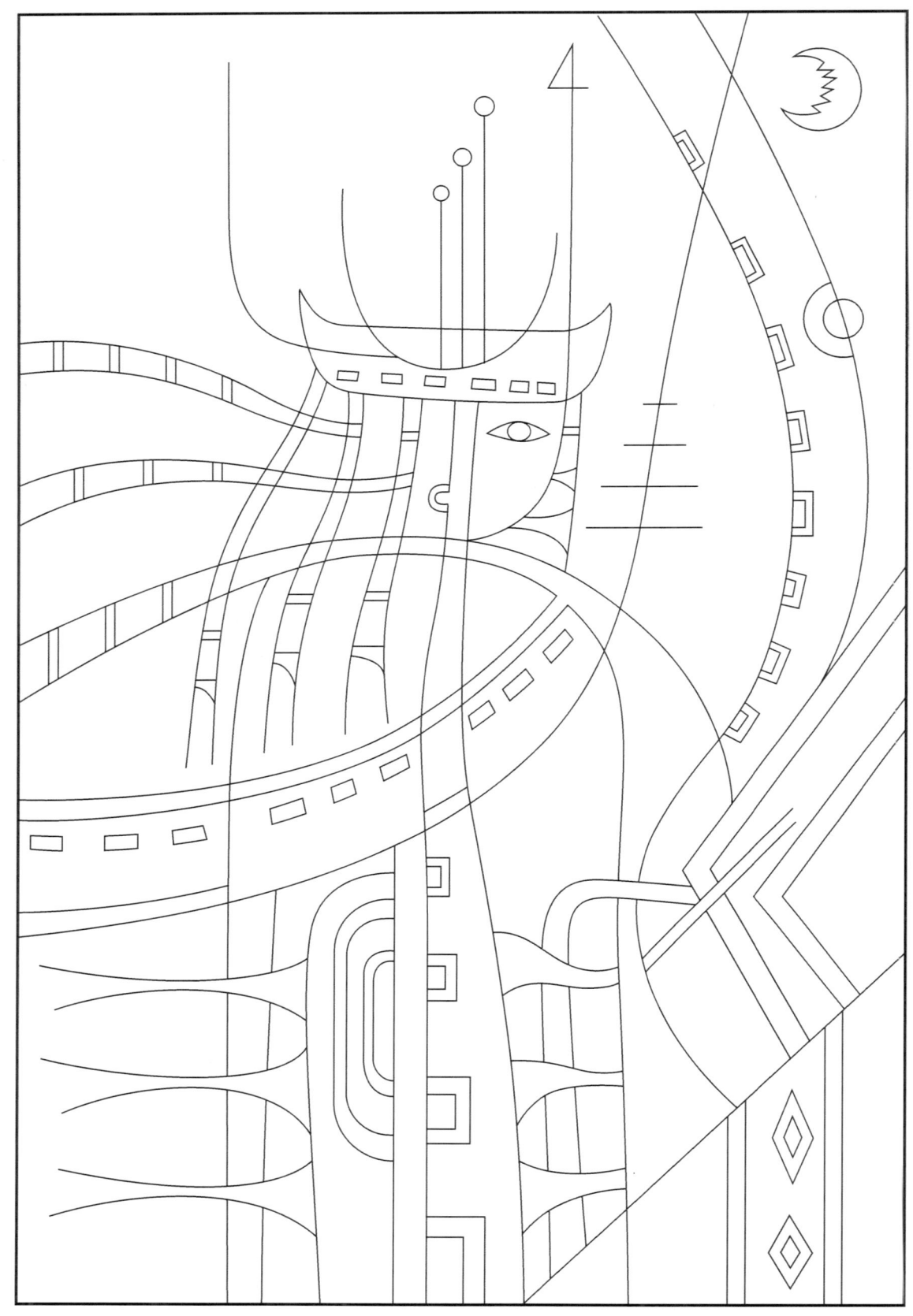

Moonlight - Tapestry 47" x 31"

Guitar at Sunset – Tapestry 55" x 19"

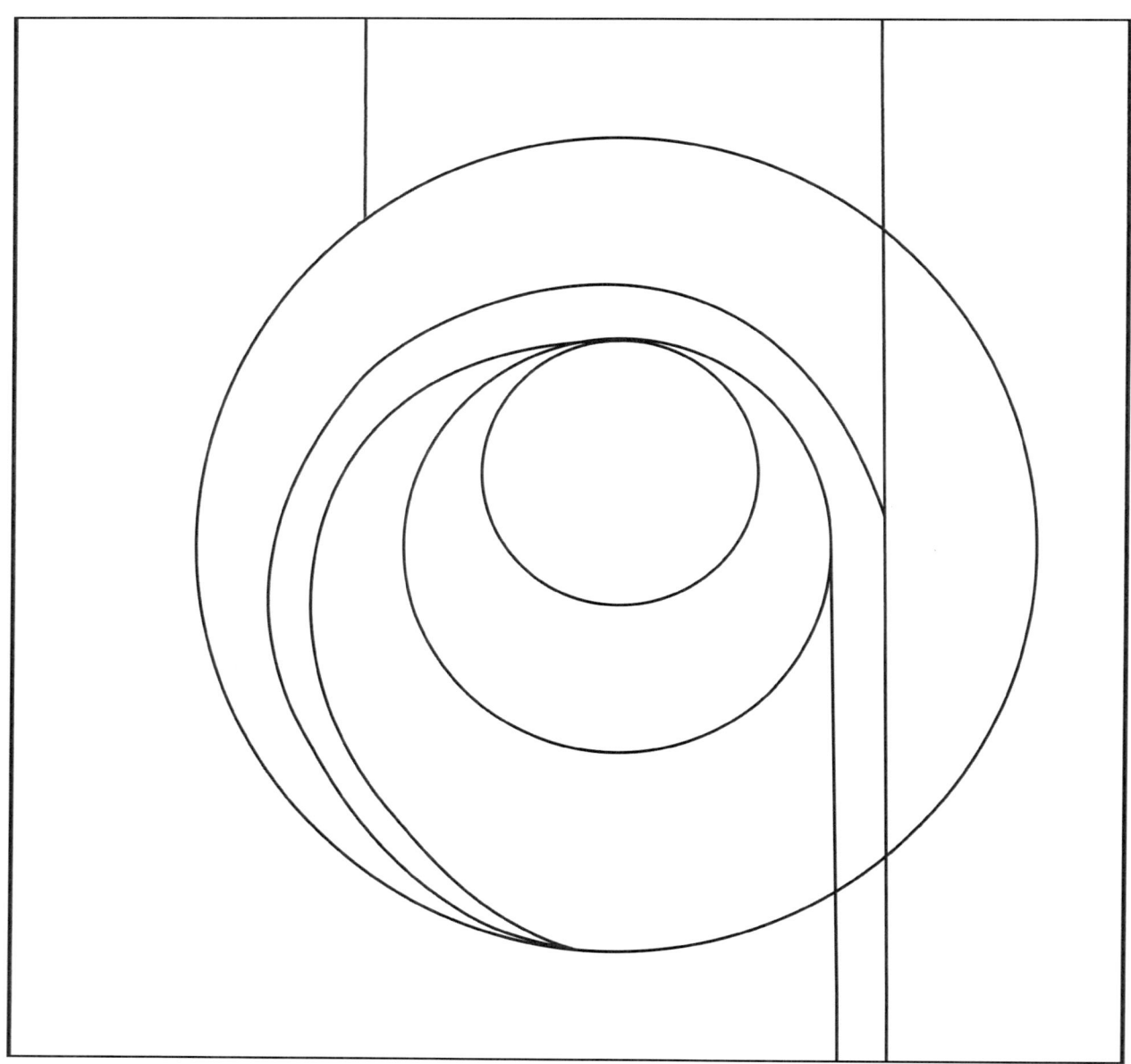

Spirit of the Jaguar II - Tapestry 47" x 47"

Fish couple – Tapestry 23" x 35"

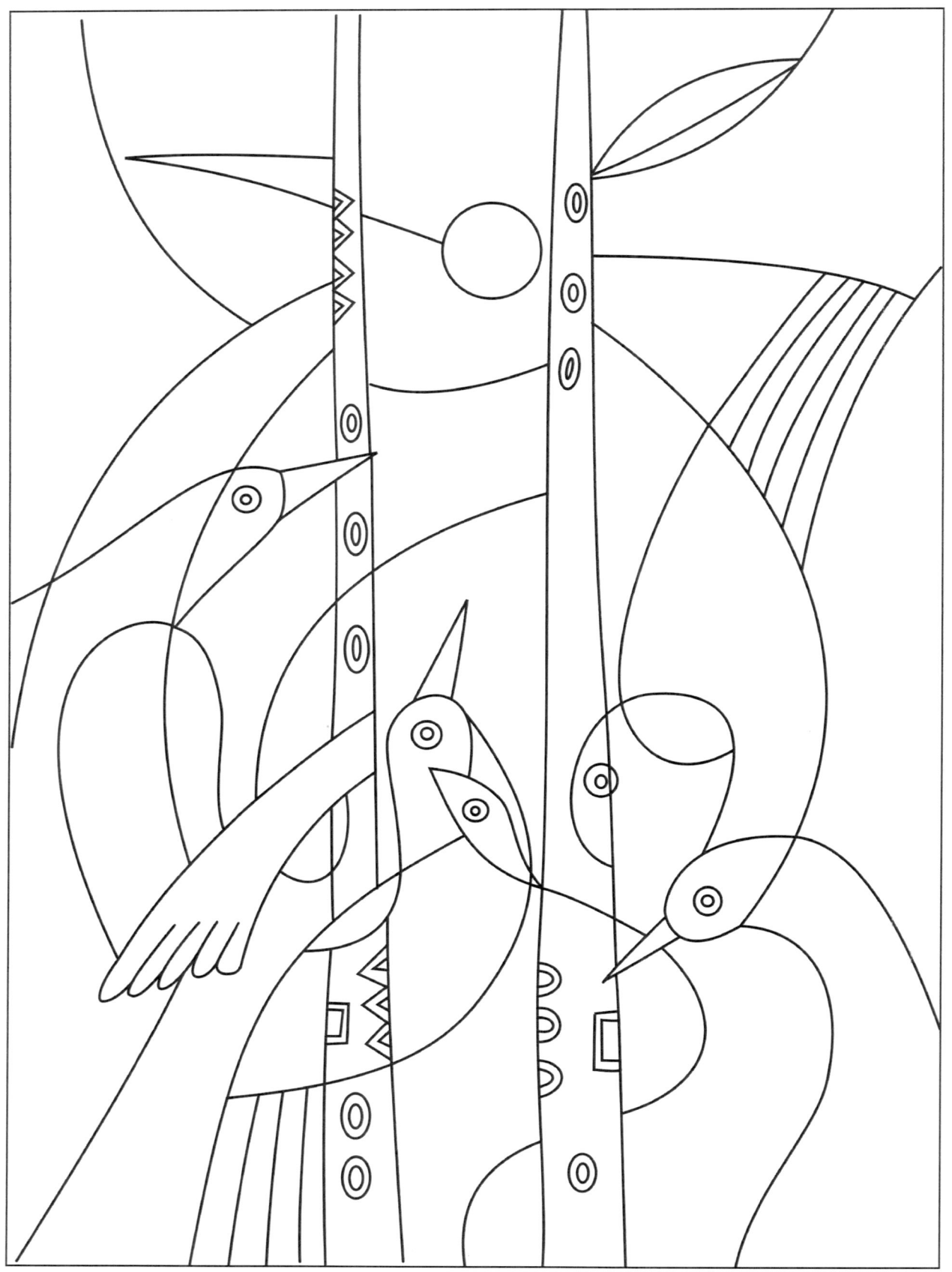

Chant for Development - Tapestry 47" x 39"

Sanctuario del Sol - Tapestry

Flight of Birds on the Field - Tapestry 47" x 47"

Some alternative colourways

Acknowledgements

This book could not have been written without the immense generosity of Máximo Laura . Not only for making his tapestry designs available but also for his encouragement for the Book project. I have also benefitted greatly from his patient teaching and his kind wisdom. It has been an enormous joy to know him and his family and to be invited into his world of colour and creativity.

Máximo's team in Lima , notably Giancarlo Soldi and Rocio Tapia, have also been extremely supportive at every stage.

Jayne Bentley Gaskins kindly allowed me to use a brilliant article she wrote for a magazine detailing the background to Máximo Laura's weaving and his Andean perspective.

Last but not least, Drew Kennedy at The Orcadian in Kirkwall, Orkney, who threw himself into the project with enthusiasm and did the layout for me. He has been a real pleasure to work with.

Rosalind Johansson

Orkney, September 2023

About the Author

Rosalind Johansson from the UK, but with deep roots in Scandinavia, pursued her creative education at Sweden's Craft Association College at Insjön in Sweden and Birmingham School of Art, UK.

She also graduated as a teacher from King Alfred's College, Winchester, part of the University of Southampton, UK, and studied International Politics at the University of Oslo, Norway.

She has enjoyed living and working in Scandinavia for 13 years, in Africa for 12 years and Peru for 18 months.

She now enjoys working from her studio in the Orkney Islands, north of Scotland.

www.ingramcontent.com/pod-product-compliance
Lightning Source LLC
Chambersburg PA
CBRC100222100526
44590CB00008B/145